DATE DUE		
FEB 11 1992		
DEC 0 8 1992		
APR 2 1 1997		
NOV 13 2001		
GAYLORD No. 2333		PRINTED IN U.S.A.

SNAKES

by Nina Leen

HOLT, RINEHART AND WINSTON / NEW YORK

I am very grateful to Dr. Herndon G. Dowling
for the time he took from his busy schedule
at New York University to help me finish this book.
Also many thanks to Marjorie Shaw,
librarian of the San Diego Zoo, for her help.

Printed in the United States of America
Layout by the author
10 9 8 7 6 5 4 3 2 1

Library of Congress Cataloging in Publication Data

Leen, Nina
  Snakes.

  Includes index.
  SUMMARY: Photographs introduce the life cycle,
behavior, and characteristics of snakes.
  1. Snakes—Juvenile literature. [1. Snakes]
I. Title.
QL666.06L43   598.1′2   77–13917
ISBN 0-03-039926-2

CONTENTS

They are not aimless wanderers.
They live in little worlds of their own.

Raymond L. Ditmars
From *Snakes of the World*

PREFACE

Raymond L. Ditmars probably more than any other person encouraged people to study and better understand reptiles, especially snakes. In his books and lectures and as Curator of Reptiles at the New York Zoological Park (Bronx Zoo), he was telling people about snakes in a manner and language that everybody could understand.

As a high-school student I was one of his ardent fans and almost a fanatic about snakes. I had practically memorized his two books, *The Reptile Book* and *Reptiles of the World*. When I finally met Dr. Ditmars he was impressed by my enthusiasm for and knowledge of snakes. Shortly after I graduated from high school I made my first trip to Cuba to collect live reptiles for exhibit at the Bronx Zoo, and preserved reptiles for the study collections of the American Museum of Natural History. From then on it was my good fortune to have R. L. Ditmars as a close friend and mentor and to be his assistant for nearly fifteen years. Even now, while working on many other projects, snakes are my favored reptiles.

Snakes have long inspired the imagination of man, but today the precise study of these reptiles is a relatively new science. The origin of snakes is still unclear since fossils are scarce. Some snakelike forms from the Cretaceous period about 135 million years ago have been found in the Sahara Desert in Africa. At present, the oldest fossil snake was found in Argentina, South America. Present thinking is that snakes probably evolved from ancient lizards, but when and how are still under discussion by scientists.

Countless misconceptions—such as: snakes hypnotize their prey; sting with their forked tongue or spiked tail; can reassemble themselves if broken in pieces; and, when danger threatens, swallow their young, later to regurgitate them unharmed. These are all pure myths that have doubtless prevented unbiased observations of snakes. This is a field where Dr. Ditmars with his widely read books was a pioneer. He refuted these and other myths to present snakes as they really are.

Snakes play an important role in the ecosystem. Of the approximately three thousand different kinds of snakes, comparatively few are deadly, the majority being nonpoisonous. Their chief economic importance is their destruction of rodents, which may carry diseases and destroy crops and stored foods. Most snakes require specialized habitats, and when these are destroyed for buildings or other types of human "progress," snakes that cannot adapt inevitably perish.

Arthur M. Greenhall, F.L.S.
Research Associate
National Museum of Natural History
Smithsonian Institution

SNAKES IN THIS BOOK

Common Name	Latin Name	Range	Venomous/ Nonvenomous	Pages
Young King Cobra	*Ophiophagus hannah*	Asia	venomous	6
Eastern Hognose Snake	*Heterodon platyrhinus*	USA	nonvenomous	12, 32, 33, 34, 35, 36, 37
Long-nosed Tree Snake	*Ahaetulla nasate*	India	venomous	13
Garter Snake	*Thamnophis sirtalis*	USA	nonvenomous	14
Desert Leaf-nosed Snake	*Phyllorhynchus decurtatus*	USA	nonvenomous	15, 23
Sharp-nosed Pit Viper	*Agkistrodon acutus*	Asia	venomous	16
Ridge-nosed Rattlesnake	*Crotalus w. willardi*	USA	venomous	17, 77
Indigo Snake	*Drymarchon corais*	USA	nonvenomous	17, 76
Eastern Diamondback Rattlesnake	*Crotalus adamanteus*	USA	venomous	18, 38, 55, 73
Yellow Rat Snake	*Elaphe absoleta quadrivittata*	USA	nonvenomous	19, 31
Anaconda	*Eunectes murinus*	South America	nonvenomous	20, 21 28, 29
Fer-de-lance	*Bothrops atrox*	Central and South America	venomous	22, 71
Florida King Snake	*Lampropeltis getulus*	USA	nonvenomous	24, 25
Western Shovel-nosed Snake	*Chionactis occipitalis annulate*	USA	nonvenomous	26, 27
Corn Snake	*Elaphe guttata*	USA	nonvenomous	30, 48, 49, 50, 51
Ground Snake	*Sonora episcopa*	USA	nonvenomous	31
Puff Adder	*Bitis arietans*	Africa	venomous	31
Water Moccasin/ Cottonmouth	*Agkistrodon piscivorus*	USA	venomous	39

Common Name	Latin Name	Range	Venomous/ Nonvenomous	Pages
Gaboon Viper	*Bitis gabonica*	Africa	venomous	40, 69
Brown Sand Boa	*Eryx johni*	India	nonvenomous	41
Twig or Bird Snake	*Thelotornis kirtlandii*	Africa	venomous	42, 43, 56
Monocled Cobra	*Naja naja kaouthis*	Indochina	venomous	44
Spectacled Cobra	*Naja naja*	India	venomous	45
Black-necked Cobra	*Naja nigricollis*	India	venomous	46, 47
European Rat Snake	*Elaphe situla*	Central Europe	nonvenomous	52, 53
Plains Garter Snake	*Thamnophis radix*	USA	nonvenomous	54
Siamese Swamp Snake	*Erpeton tentaculatum*	Asia	nonvenomous	56
African Egg-Eater	*Dasypeltis scaber*	Africa	nonvenomous	57, 58, 59, 60, 61
California King Snake	*Lampropeltis getulus*	USA	nonvenomous	62, 63, 64, 65
Pacific Rattlesnake	*Crotalus viridis oreganus*	USA	venomous	62, 63 64, 65
Green Tree Python	*Chondropython viridis*	New Guinea	nonvenomous	66
Emerald Tree Boa	*Corallus caninus*	So. America	nonvenomous	67
Rhinoceros Viper	*Bitis nasicornis*	Africa	venomous	68
Death Adder	*Acanthophis antarcticus*	Australia	venomous	70
Common Coral Snake	*Micrurus f. fulvius*	USA	venomous	72
Scarlet King Snake	*Lampropeltis trianculum elapsoides*	USA	nonvenomous	72
Water Cobra	*Boulengerina annulata*	Africa	venomous	74
King Cobra	*Ophiophagus hannah*	Asia	venomous	75
San Francisco Garter Snake	*Thamnophis sirtalis tetrataenis*	USA	nonvenomous	77

FOREWORD

Why do snakes—mute, deaf, without arms and legs, usually much smaller than a human—frighten people out of their wits? Is it their way of life, a soundless appearance from nowhere, a starry look in their perpetually open eyes, swift movement without visible means of locomotion?

Whatever it is, the snake is shrouded in mystery and superstition. It is the most intensely hated and feared animal, yet it is admired for its beauty. Thousands of years ago, people admired the beauty of snakes, their graceful movements, the colors and designs of their skin. Snake sculptures, paintings, and precious figurines were worshiped as symbols of life and reincarnation. Even in this century, snakes are kept as guardians of family homes and villages in some countries. Perhaps the snakes' diet of rodents has something to do with it.

Tales of snakes milking cows (snakes dislike milk!), hypnotizing people, stinging with their tongue, or "crushing humans to a pulp" are fantasies born of ignorance and fear. Snakes don't deserve their bad reputation: Most of them are harmless, they don't look for human companionship, they prefer to be left alone. The old myth that the snake's body is slimy and cold is believed by people who have never touched a snake. The skin of a snake is dry, smooth, and looks highly "polished," but it is not slimy. I have handled snakes, I've had some of my own, but I never found a snake to be slippery or wet—except when it came out of the water.

Snakes are different from all other animals—and even from other reptiles. They won't come when called, because they can't hear. They don't sing, bark, meow, or cry in pain, because they have no voice. Since it is quite difficult to communicate with them, it is up to the human to show understanding. A human who is frightened should know enough to retreat—instead of killing a snake on sight.

Today people do not worship serpents. But they do go to the zoo in great numbers and stand transfixed in the reptile house watching the fascinating snake. Even people who hate snakes cannot help going to those exhibits.

I like the phrase from Ralph Waldo Emerson "Fear always springs from ignorance"—it could be applied to *ophidiophobia,* the fear of snakes.

N. L.

Senses

Snakes have the same senses man has—only they function differently. Additional highly specialized organs equip snakes for their unusual way of life.

Snakes' eyes are unique. No other animal has such eyes. They have no eyelids and their eyes are always open. For protection, a transparent lens called a "spectacle" covers the eye. The absence of eyelids makes the *Eastern hognose snake* appear to be staring.

Many snakes with eyes set far apart on either side of their heads are not able to see ahead of themselves. This Indian *long-nosed tree snake* is one of the few exceptions. A groove from the eye to the nose makes it possible for it to look with both eyes forward.

Looking at the frog with one eye, the *garter snake* ignores its prey—so long as the frog does not move. Most snakes are shortsighted. They detect movement but may not recognize nonmoving objects close by.

The *desert leaf-nosed snake* roams around at night. As in many other nocturnal animals, the pupils of its eyes are vertical. The unusual leaf in front of its nose is probably helpful when it burrows in sand during the day.

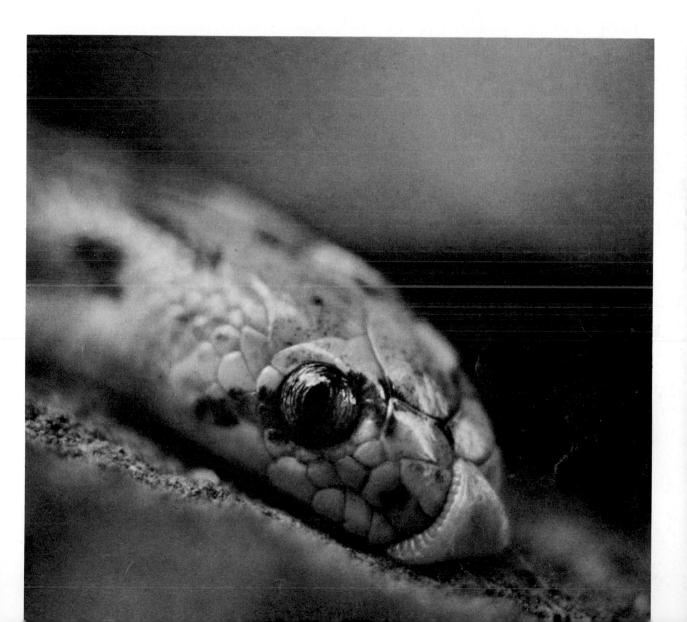

Like all snakes, the *sharp-nosed pit viper* is deaf—it has no external ear, no eardrum, and no middle ear. But, like man, it has an inner ear. And it can "hear" vibrations transmitted through the ground. Pit vipers and rattlers have a facial pit (sometimes mistaken for an ear), an opening between the eyes and the nostrils. An unusual sense organ, it is sensitive to heat and helps the snake detect a predator or follow warm-blooded prey.

With flickering tongues, the *ridge-nosed rattlesnake* (above) and the *indigo snake* (below) explore everything around them. The snake "smells" with its tongue as well as its nose. The tongue has no sense of taste and is not a "stinger"—it is totally harmless. But for the snake it is the most important part of its anatomy. With the forks of its tongue, the snake picks up invisible particles from air and ground and places them in Jacobson's organ—two small cavities in the roof of its mouth. There the particles are analyzed and the snake is informed about its surroundings.

Habitat

Snakes live everywhere in the world except New Zealand, Ireland, some isolated oceanic islands, and polar regions. Their habitat is varied: They live on the ground, in trees, in water, in woods, and in sand. Most snakes inhabit the tropics—warm temperatures and year-round abundance of food are good reasons for this.

The *Eastern diamond-back rattlesnake* lives in sparsely populated parts of the brush country in the southeastern U.S. It favors places abundant with low-growing palmetto palms.

The *yellow rat snake* is often seen resting in trees but sometimes it is found on the ground. A good climber, it looks for birds and bird eggs in tree branches. To hunt rodents or small mammals it comes down.

Water is habitat for many snakes. Even terrestrial snakes are known to go swimming. The *South American anaconda*, the world's largest snake, is semiaquatic; it prefers to be in water—in rivers and swamps. It feeds on a variety of fishes, but when a more substantial meal is desired the anaconda settles down on a riverbank.

At water's edge, well camouflaged, anacondas wait patiently for fowl or mammals to pass close by or approach the water for a drink. The prey—deer, sheep, peccaries, and large rodents—is seized, constricted, and eaten. If the meal was large enough, weeks, even months can pass until the snake is hungry again. Anacondas seem to like each other's company. Two or more are often seen resting together.

Decayed tree stumps in wet forests of Central and South America are favored haunts of the *fer-de-lance*. Occasionally it ventures into the open country, around human settlements, and into cultivated fields to hunt rats—a special treat.

Many species of snakes live in the desert. During the day, rocks, bushes, crevices, and burrows offer shelter from sun and heat. At dawn the *desert leaf-nosed snake* goes underground in soft sand and seldom comes up before nightfall.

Locomotion

Snakes move in many different ways. They crawl, wiggle, climb, swim, and burrow themselves in sand and earth.

The *Florida king snake* is crossing from tree to tree on a vine high above the ground.

Most snakes are able to use a variety of propulsions—whatever movement is best suited to a situation.

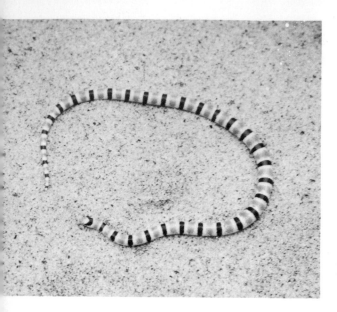

Sand–swimmers are small snakes inhabiting wild parts of the desert. They are so named because they "swim" fast and easily in sand below the surface. Spending their life under the sand, they appear at night and are seldom seen by people.

The *Western shovel-nosed snake* starts its disappearing act.

Head first, it speedily wiggles itself into the sand, sinking deeper and deeper, disappearing in seconds.

All snakes can swim, but the giant *anaconda* spends most of its life in water. It can hold its breath for several minutes before lifting its head above the water for air. Its size and life-style make this giant a favored part of South American folklore. Reports of hundred-foot long monstrous anacondas, roaming the rivers and devouring everything and everybody in sight, are heard from time to time. Those tales are exciting but they are not true.

Without limbs or wings, the snake can propel itself to any destination. The four predominant techniques are sidewinding, serpentine wriggle, caterpillar crawl, and concertina movement. The snake sometimes combines several locomotions to cover a terrain.

The *corn snake* uses the concertina propulsion to climb up a tree.

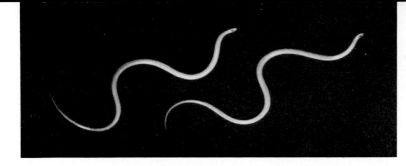

Double exposure of
a *ground snake* in
sidewinding locomotion.

This multiple-exposure photograph shows a *rat snake* using the
serpentine technique. It wriggles forward in S-curves, using the
slightest irregularities on the ground as points of resistance
against sliding backward.

Heavy-bodied snakes, like the *puff adder*, often use the
caterpillar crawl. Sections of the belly scales expand and contract
as the snake moves forward in a straight line.

31

Defense for Survival

Defense is the most important part of the snake's life. Man and many other mammals, birds, reptiles, and even other snakes are dangerous enemies. They are to be avoided or fooled. Ingenious ways of defense help snakes to survive.

The harmless *Eastern hognose* has the most remarkable defensive behavior. When threatened, it spreads a hood, bloats its body, hisses, rises, convulses, and plays dead.

If approached, it will suddenly flop on its back pretending to be dead. After some time it slowly turns to see whether the enemy has gone. If danger is still present, it will flop back again to prove that it's still dead.

It can flip over on its back with lightning speed—so quickly that even the smallest leaves on the ground around its body are not disturbed. The snake loses this unique defense behavior in captivity.

Doing its best to look frightening, the *black hognose* rises as if imitating the feared cobra—although the two snakes live many thousands of miles apart.

The head of the hognose when it is not alarmed is no wider than its body.

When disturbed it can flatten its head and neck to more than twice the original size.

To scare away the persistent intruder, the hognose inflates its lungs and blows air out with a loud hiss. It opens a gaping mouth and lunges at the enemy—a very convincing performance.

Shaking the horny coils at the end of its tail, the *Eastern diamondback rattlesnake* gives audible warning of its presence. The sound protects the snake from being stepped on by larger creatures or molested by its enemies.

The *cottonmouth* or *water moccasin* lives in the southeastern United States. It has an inoffensive disposition and rarely moves away when disturbed. Instead, it opens a gaping, white mouth to frighten the intruder. It is a sluggish but very dangerous snake—its bite can be lethal.

Camouflaged on the ground of the tropical rain forest in Africa, the *gaboon viper* is hard to detect. The colors and pattern of its skin blending perfectly with fallen leaves, the snake is easily overlooked by enemies.

The *brown sand boa* is a small Indian snake, about two and a half feet long. Some natives call it the "two-headed snake." The reason is obvious—both ends look alike. The enemy will often bite the tail, the false "head," and fail to kill the snake. The little boa is nonpoisonous. The natural deception is its only defense.

The *twig snake* in Africa lives mostly in trees. The slender snake blends well with vines and twigs. The forepart of the body can remain motionless, suspended in the air, as its eyes follow an intruder. Like other tree snakes, the twig snake can look forward and recognize nonmoving potential danger or prey.

When threatened, it inflates its neck, exposing the skin between the scales. A dark design resembling a giant eye appears to bluff away the enemy. If this deception fails, the snake will strike with a most effective venom.

When confronted by danger, the *monocled cobra* from Indochina
flattens the skin of its neck over widely spread long ribs. The
stretched skin reveals a weird "mask" that is supposed to
intimidate the enemy.

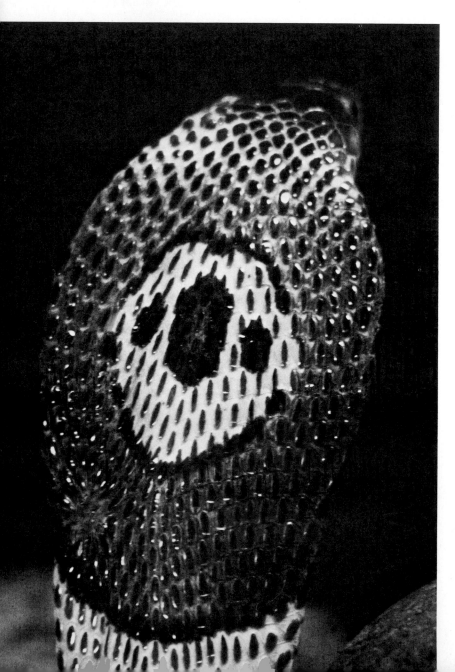

The warning of the
Indian spectacled cobra
is the appearance of
a grotesque face wearing
spectacles on the back
of its spread hood.

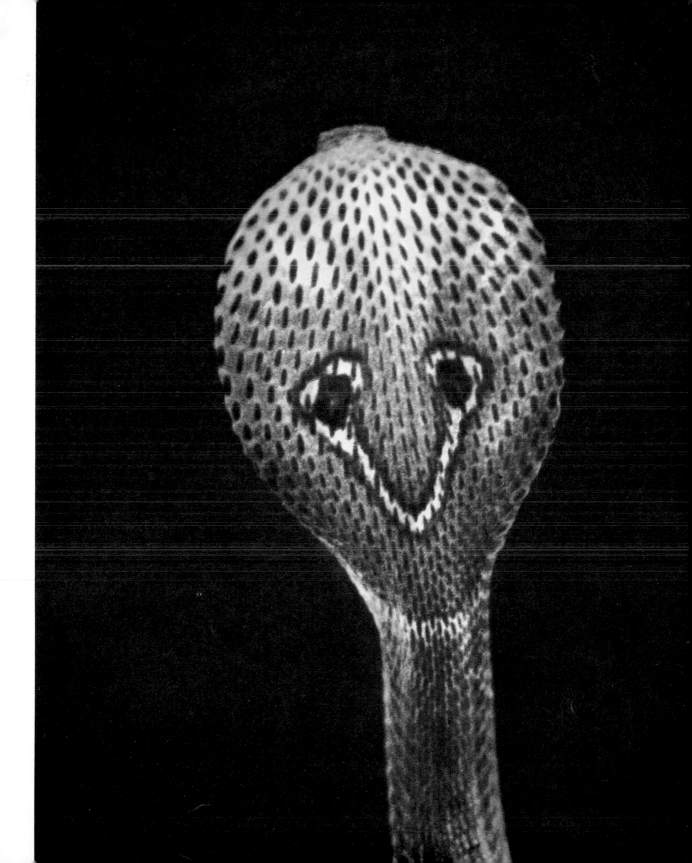

A *spitting cobra* uses its deadly aim only defensively. The *black-necked cobra* of Africa, which can spit poison, aims at the eyes of an aggressor as far as eight feet away. The spray is emitted through pinholes on the front of its fangs. The poison can cause pain, eye damage, or permanent blindness.

Droplets of poison just ejected are visible in this photograph, the only still picture ever taken to show the spitting.

A Corn Snake Is Hatched

Most snakes lay eggs and abandon them as soon as they are laid. The mother deposits the eggs in a rotting log, decaying vegetation, or similar location, well hidden from intruders. The egg continues to grow until the snake inside it is fully developed. The unborn baby gets nourishment from the yolk till it's ready to hatch. When the time comes, the hatchling uses an "egg tooth" to cut through the tough, leathery eggshell. Baby snakes seem to enjoy slashing their way to the outside; several cuts can be seen in the empty, collapsed shells.

The tip of a snout appears through the open slit in the eggshell. Then comes the head, to take a first look around, but it quickly disappears inside the egg again. Newborn snakes do not have to leave the egg at once. They stay on for a few days, living on the remains of the yolk they are still digesting.

The egg is their home and they are in no hurry to move out. The egg shrivels when the fluid starts to seep out, but this seems not to bother the baby. It is surprising how much snake can fit into a small egg—a 15-inch baby snake in a 1½-inch egg!

When the young snake leaves the egg it is alone in the world. No mother guides or protects it. The newborn has to hunt for food and face danger. The hatchlings in one bunch may have different dispositions—some are shy but most of them are full of courage and ready to defend themselves the moment they leave the egg. This inborn defense behavior may be nature's way to help them to survive.

European Rat-Snake Shedding

There are no rules for when a snake should or should not shed its skin. It probably depends on how much the snake moves around and how fast it wears out the old skin. Air temperature may also be a factor. About ten days before shedding, the snake becomes listless. It stops eating, the eyes cloud over, it cannot see and usually goes into hiding. Before shedding, an oily secretion loosens the old skin and the snake can actually peel it off. The snake skin is shed in one piece. The snake starts pushing the skin off at its jaws by rubbing against a rough surface. Moving against rocks, logs, or tree branches, it crawls out of it, exposing a bright, shiny new skin.

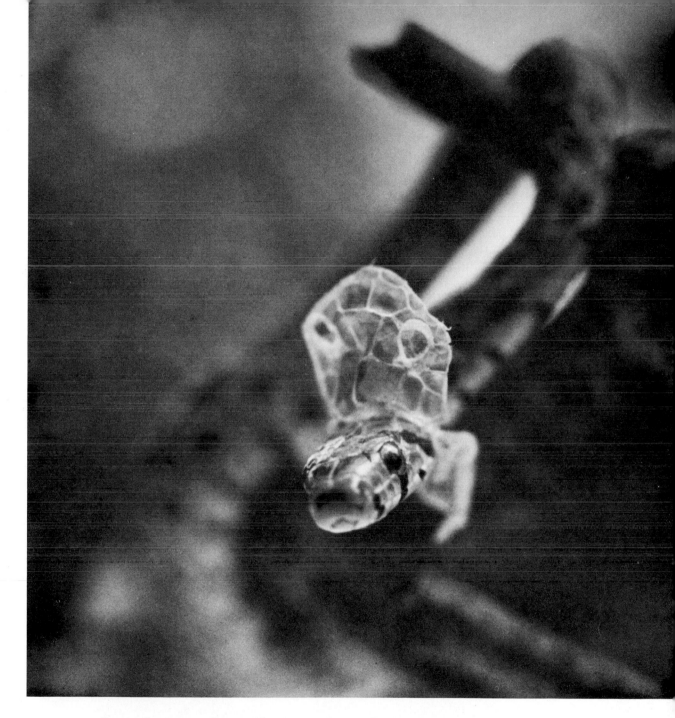

In early times the snake was admired, worshiped, and envied for its ability to "renew its youth." Because of its continuing shedding, many ancient legends and writings described the snake as immortal—never growing old or dying.

Temperature

Extreme heat or temperatures below freezing are fatal to the
snake. Unlike mammals and birds, snakes cannot control their
internal body heat; they have to depend on the temperature
outside to warm or cool them. They generate so little heat inside
their bodies that most snakes will not survive freezing. In
climates with cold winters they have to find places to hibernate
protected from frost. Through the right behavior they are able to
keep their body temperature stable: On cool days they rest in
warming sun or move around to raise their body heat, on hot days
they hide in cool places.

In spring, a clump of *Plains garter snakes* entwine themselves
after hibernating deep under rocks, shielded from icy winds and
freezing cold. Often many snakes huddle together to hibernate.

The *Eastern diamondback rattlesnake* hides from the hot sun in the shade of a dwarf palmetto leaf.

Unusual Eating Habits

The *African twig snake* uses its brightly colored tongue as a lure to attract prey.

A coat of algae covers the *Siamese swamp snake*. It never leaves fresh water. The algae coat is a welcome camouflage—it fools the **little fish that the snake eats.**

A snake's diet often includes prey many times larger than its mouth and body. The snake would starve to death if nature had not provided an ingenious jaw construction that makes it possible for the snake to stretch its mouth way out of proportion to its body. The snake does not eat and swallow food with the help of its tongue, as mammals do. Instead, it pulls itself over the prey and consumes it slowly, and in one piece.

The *African egg-eater* approaches its favored food. Many snakes eat eggs, but this snake eats nothing but eggs.

The size of the egg does not discourage the *African egg-eater*.

It can stretch the loosely connected jaws wider than any other snake can to swallow an egg twice as thick as its own body.

Encircling the egg with its
body, the snake prevents the
egg from rolling around.
Then, securing a firm grip, it
stretches its mouth to the limit
and starts the laborious task of
drawing itself over the egg.
The skin of the neck becomes
extremely distended, giving
the snake a bizarre
appearance.

The egg moves down the throat, where it is pierced by sharp spines. Squeezed by neck muscles, the egg suddenly collapses, releasing its contents to run down to the stomach.

The snake starts to spit out the empty eggshell. When a large meal blocks its mouth, muscles push its windpipe forward just enough to make breathing possible. (The round opening of the windpipe is seen in the picture.)

Finally, drained of its fluids, the empty, compressed eggshell is regurgitated by the snake.

A nonpoisonous *California king snake* meets the *Pacific rattler*—its next meal.

Snakes eat snakes, but the most consistent snake eater is the *king snake*. Because the prey is eaten in one piece, an ideal shape for a snake to swallow is another snake. The rattler's venom is useless against this aggressor—the king snake is immune to it. Sensing the danger, with no escape possible, the rattler tries with an "elbow" to push away the enemy.

With a quick move the king snake loops itself around the rattler. Squeezed by strong coils, the rattler looses its last resistance and dies.

When the prey is dead, the king snake is ready to start its meal. The head is always swallowed first.

When the swallowing begins, a flow of saliva lubricates the victim's body. Even though the long rattler is conveniently shaped, it's still a slow, tiresome task for the king snake to ingest it.

The king snake takes a short rest before the last of the rattlesnake is swallowed. The meal lasted about one hour.

Constrictors

This name applies to nonpoisonous giant snakes—the boas, pythons, anacondas, and their relatives. Small snakes constrict their victims too, but they are not called constrictors. The constrictor strikes at its prey, then holds it tight in its jaws as it coils around the prey, squeezing until the victim stops struggling.

LEFT. The *green tree python*, at home only in New Guinea, is protected there by the government. A small relative of the giant pythons, it lives in trees and is seldom seen by people. It hunts mostly at night.

RIGHT. The *emerald tree boa* from South America lives in the treetops of the tropical forest. It feeds mostly on birds, squirrels, and iguana lizards. A row of heat-sensing pits between its jaws helps the boa to locate its prey.

Hunting with Poison

Subduing a prey, the limbless snake can be badly injured. The victim is not defenseless—it can fight with teeth, claws, horns, hoofs, even quills. The most effective weapon a snake has is poison. After a quick strike, the snake waits for the injected venom to kill. When the victim no longer shows resistance, the snake starts swallowing, head first.

The highly venomous *rhinoceros viper* lives in Africa. It is often seen along riverbanks, crawling in or out of the water. An exquisite butterfly design in tones predominantly of blue and yellow covers its body.

The *gaboon viper* in Africa has the unique distinction of being the fattest, heaviest, and probably the most beautiful poisonous snake. Its design resembles more an artful weaving than the skin of a snake. Considered a good-natured snake, though dangerously venomous, it prefers to escape from trouble. But if cornered, it will puff up, hiss, and lunge, sinking two-inch fangs into the enemy.

The *death adder* is a serpent rarity. A short snake with a heavy body and a triangular head with long fangs, it looks like an adder, but it is not. There are no adders in Australia. The death adder is an elapid, a member of the cobra family.

A venomous record-breaker in Australia, the mortality rate of its victims is 50 percent. Because its bite lasts longer it injects more poison into the wound. The death adder is considered the largest venom producer among Australian snakes.

Fer-de-lance is the most feared snake in Central and South America. Its poison causes major damage in the victim's body and painful death if serum is not immediately available. It spends the day in a hollow, damp tree trunk, emerging at night to hunt.

The poisonous *common coral snake* of the southern United States (right) and its look-alike, the nonpoisonous *scarlet king snake* (left). Some harmless mimics of the coral snake are often killed by people because of mistaken identity. Common coral snakes have a very potent venom. Their behavior is secretive. When encountered, they usually will not bite people except in desperation. They should never be touched with bare hands. Their diet consists mainly of other snakes— the scarlet king snake is one of them.

It is easy to recognize the real coral snake if the following is kept in mind: The colors of both snakes are red, black, and yellow, but the arrangement is different. If *red touches yellow* and the *snout is black*—it's the real coral snake.

Eastern diamondback rattlesnake is the largest venomous snake in North America. It hunts rabbits, small mammals, and occasional birds. With its powerful poison it can kill a gopher in a minute. The rattler is sluggish and not belligerent, but if confronted by an enemy it will stay and fight.

RIGHT. *King cobra* of Asia has the majesty of a king among serpents. It is the longest poisonous snake and has extremely toxic venom. It is also considered to be the most intelligent of all snakes. It makes a nest for its eggs and guards them until the young hatch. The king cobra feeds mostly on snakes, including cobras. Its Latin generic name, *Ophiaphagus*, means snake eater.

The *African water cobra* lives in the lakes of Central Africa. These snakes feed on fishes and appear to be nonaggressive. But it is safer to leave them alone as no antivenin exists for their poison.

Endangered Snakes

Some snakes are becoming vanishing species as their habitats are destroyed to make space for roads and houses. Others are over collected by dealers and pet hunters. Countless are killed because they are poisonous—or people assume that they are. These three snakes are protected by the U.S. government and appear on its List of Endangered Species.

The black, glassy *indigo snake* is a favorite with snake collectors. It is found in the southeastern United States.

The small *ridge-nosed rattlesnake* has a very limited range. It lives in the extreme southern part of Arizona.

The *San Francisco garter snake* inhabits only the peninsula south of San Francisco.

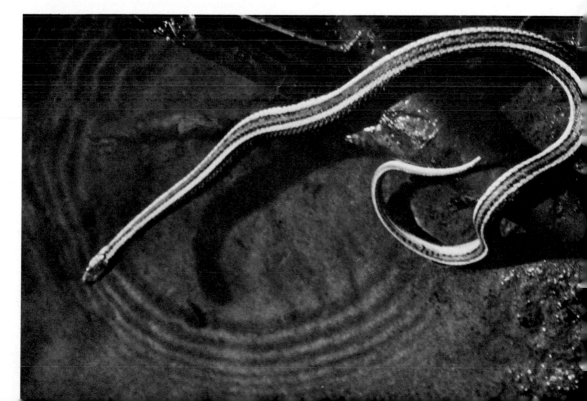

SUGGESTED READING

Ditmars, R. L. *Snakes of the World.* New York: Macmillan, 1932.

Ditmars, R. L. *Reptiles of the World.* New York: Macmillan, 1966.

Harrison, H. H. *The World of the Snake.* New York: J. B. Lippincott, 1971.

Kauffeld, C. *Snakes: The Keeper and the Kept.* Garden City, N.Y.: Doubleday, 1969.

Life Nature Library. *The Reptiles.* New York: Time Inc., 1963.

Morris, Ramona and Desmond. *Men and Snakes.* New York: McGraw-Hill, 1965.

Poisonous Snakes of the World. A Manual for Use by U.S. Amphibious Forces, Department of the Navy, United States Government Printing Office, Washington, D.C. 20402.

Pope, C. H. *The Giant Snakes.* New York: Alfred A. Knopf, 1961.

Pope, C. H. *The Reptile World.* New York: Alfred A. Knopf, 1971.

Schmidt, K. P., and Davis, D. D. *Field Book of Snakes of the U.S. and Canada.* New York: G. P. Putnam's Sons, 1944.

Schmidt, K. P., and Inger, R. F. *Living Reptiles of the World.* Garden City, N.Y.: Doubleday, 1957.

Shaw, C. E., and Campbell, S. *Snakes of the American West.* New York: Alfred A. Knopf, 1974.

Stidworthy, J. *Snakes of the World.* New York: Bantam, 1972.

Time-Life Films. *Reptiles and Amphibians.* New York: Time Inc., 1976.

INDEX